Way Maker

AN ADVENT STUDY THROUGH THE BOOK OF HEBREWS

By
Erin H. Warren

Copyright © 2020, 2021, 2022, 2023 by Erin H. Warren
Published by Headley Warren Productions LLC
Orlando, Florida
www.FeastingOnTruth.com

ISBN 978-1-959305-12-5

contents

start here

If I had designed the ancient temple in Jerusalem, I would have created beautiful marble steps leading up it. You know, like the ones leading up to the great libraries or monuments. But that's not how the steps leading to the temple in Jerusalem were built. The steps leading up to the temple are all different lengths, heights, and depths. It may look like an accident, but it was designed this way on purpose. The mismatched steps force temple visitors to look down, watch their step, and enter with reverence. One couldn't easily run up the steps and rush into the temple. They had to do so with intention.

That is how I view Advent: a season to slow down and take in the wonder and miracle of Jesus' birth; a season of reflection and anticipation. The word *advent* comes from the Latin word *adventus* which means "coming". Traditionally, it started as believers looked toward the Second Coming of Christ, but over time it has come to include not only His birth at Christmas, but our coming to Him for salvation as well. While my Advent typically doesn't look like a traditional Advent (one year I bought candles, determined to light them, but never bought candle holders, so . . .), I do make a habit of approaching the season as worshippers would approach the temple: slowly, intentionally, and reverently.

I feel like we often love to focus on the sweet Baby Jesus, lying there in a manger, wrapped in pure white cloths, with stars all around, and animals quietly lying down next to Him. But over the years, I've come to view Christmas through the eye of Easter. Easter was His purpose for coming to begin with, so Christmas and Easter will forever be intertwined. Philippians 2:5–8 says:

> *Have this mind among yourselves, which is yours in Christ Jesus, who, though he was in the form of God, did not count equality with God a thing to be grasped, but emptied himself, by taking the form of a servant, being born in the likeness of men. And being found in human form, he humbled himself by becoming obedient to the point of death, even death on a cross.*

He humbly took all of His God power and constrained it into the form of a baby. He came down. To us. Not as a great king, but as a servant. And He died on the cross. For us.

I think sometimes we only preach half the gospel; we focus on John 3:16. And that sounds like a great deal for us. We made the mistake; Jesus paid the price. We get to go to heaven. But Jesus' coming was so much more than that.

Without Jesus, we were condemned, destined for death and hell, separated from God, both now and for eternity (John 3:17). Jesus came not only to provide a way to eternal life in heaven with Him, but so that we might be able to dwell in His presence, both now and forever. He came to restore the broken relationship between us and God.

He did not come to make life easy. No, His coming was the greatest act of humility. Because He loves us so much.

I want to spend this Advent season remembering Him this way. And there's no greater book to show us how Jesus made a way than the book of Hebrews.

WHY HEBREWS?

In Exodus, as the Israelites were wandering in the wilderness, God gave them a way for Him to dwell in their midst. God is holy, and we are not. In order for us to have communion with a holy, pure, righteous God, we must be made clean. God provided this way through a sacrificial system in the Tabernacle. Through a series of sacrifices, cleansing, and prayers, the priests would go before God on behalf of the people. They interceded for the people. This continued for hundreds of years, eventually moving to the permanent temple in Jerusalem; but then came Jesus. He did what the blood of bulls and goats could not do: He finished the work once and for all.

Hebrews is a book written to show how Jesus is the fulfillment of the law. The author uses the word *shadow*—that these things are not the true form but instead point us to truth. In fact, if you trace the steps through the Tabernacle, they form the shape of a cross. Hebrews is often called the fifth gospel, and no other book gives us a more concise picture of what Jesus did in making a way for us.

CONTEXT

Anytime we prepare to study a book of the Bible, it's important to set the lens through which we study. The Bible is a book written for us, but we were not the original audience. It helps us better interpret Scripture when we understand first and foremost what it meant to the original audience.

We do not know who wrote the book of Hebrews, but we know it was written around 68 AD, before the destruction of the temple in 70 AD. The Greeks during this time in history would start their letters or persuasive speeches by establishing their own credibility. This is why Paul's letters often start with "Paul, a servant of Christ." Paul was stating why the recipients of his letter should listen.

In contrast, the author of Hebrews wasn't trying to establish who he was, but rather who Jesus was and why they should look to Jesus:

> *Long ago, at many times and in many ways, God spoke to our fathers by*
> *the prophets, but in these last days he has spoken to us by his Son, whom he*
> *appointed the heir of all things, through whom also he created the world. He is*
> *the radiance of the glory of God and the exact imprint of his nature, and he up-*
> *holds the universe by the word of his power. After making purification for sins,*

he sat down at the right hand of the Majesty on high, having become as much
superior to angels as the name he has inherited is more excellent than theirs.
Hebrews 1:1–4

I love that the author doesn't name himself. It's like saying, "It's not about me. It's about Him." He starts with Jesus.

This was a time of intense persecution in the church. Nero was emperor of the Roman Empire and he was known for his persecution of Christians. In 64 AD, it grew to its height as he blamed Christians for the burning of Rome. Tensions between Jewish religious leaders and Christians were high, and I can imagine doubts among this new church may have been rising as well. The author of Hebrews wrote these words to encourage Jewish Christians and remind them of who Jesus is and what He did. He was calling them (and us) to move forward and not turn back.

THE PLAN

I'm embarrassed to tell you how many unfinished Advent books I have. It's such a busy season with so many activities, and it usually doesn't take long for me to fall behind. So, I wanted this journal, this guide through Hebrews, to be doable for Advent. There are thirteen readings, each between four to ten verses. You can do them in thirteen days or, as I like to do, linger in each passage for a couple of days. Take two days to meditate on the verses and listen to them in your car while driving. Do not worry about cramming it in before Christmas. Technically, the Christmas season doesn't end until Epiphany on January 6.

My passion is to encourage and equip women to discover God's truths in Scripture for themselves. Because of that, I want to keep this book simple, not focusing on my words, but helping guide you toward the simple truths of who God is in the book of Hebrews. Each day consists of four simple actions:

Write it out.

I love writing Scripture! There's something so powerful in writing out verses as I study. I pay attention to each word and often catch things I would otherwise miss. I encourage you to read the entire chapter, but focus on the selected verses.

What does this tell us about Jesus?

The Bible is not a book about us; it's a book about Him. His character is written across every page, in every verse. Take a few moments to jot down the characteristics of God you see here. To help you, I have a list of names and characteristics of God on pages 12–13. I know there are some separate roles for each person of the Trinity, but to keep things simple, this list includes God the Father, God the Son, and God the Holy Spirit.

How is He the Way Maker?

Read the selected verses—how does this tell us how Jesus made a way for us? Remember, it's not only about making a way through life, but a way to relationship with our Heavenly Father.

Write a prayer of thanksgiving for who He is.

We often come to God with our requests, but I want to focus on thanking Him this Advent season. No matter what we are going through, there is always something to be thankful for. I love to focus this prayer of thanksgiving on the characteristics of God in that particular passage.

(Optional) Go Deeper questions

Hebrews is a deep book, and we could spend hours diving into the truths written in these verses. If you have time and want to—go for it! These questions will help you go further in your study, and there is space to add your own notes on the chapter as well.

Remember

In the back of the book on page 107, you'll find a section to remember and reflect back on this year. This is one of my favorite practices at the end of the year. It's important to look back over the year, to recognize the places where you saw God move, and to see His character on display. There's also a place to look forward to the coming year. We are commanded again and again in Scripture to remember. I encourage you to find a quiet moment before the New Year to go through those questions. Pray, and ask the Holy Spirit to help you remember (it's His job—John 14:26).

Devotionals

Throughout the book, I included devotionals for some of the passages from Hebrews. Several years ago, my family went through a crisis as my husband was diagnosed with an autoimmune disease (Praise God; he is doing well!). Many of these words were written during the hardship of that year, especially that Christmas. I was facing feelings of fear, a loss of control, unmet expectations, and I found myself overwhelmed by all of it.

> *But Jesus.*
> He never left me.
> He never let me go.
> His light was never overcome.
> He does the same for you.

COMPANION TEACHINGS AND OTHER RESOURCES

Companion teachings for this study are available on Season 6 of the Feasting on Truth podcast. In each episode I provide cultural commentary, insight from the original language, and guidance in how to study the meaning behind the passages. My desire is to walk alongside you as you learn to have a God-centered approach to Scripture. It's not as hard as it seems! To simplify your study time, I've put together a series of emails with direct links to the podcast teachings for that week of Advent, so you won't have to hunt for them! All you need to do is scan the QR code or visit FeastingOnTruth.com/WayMaker to sign up.

I am so excited for you this Advent season. I want you to know that I am praying for you. I am praying that the Holy Spirit will meet you as you read and you will start the year with renewed faith in our Way Maker. I pray that this season is a time of slow, intentional, reverent time with Jesus.

Because of Christ,

Erin H. Warren

simple Christmas

I collapsed onto the couch and stared at my bare Christmas tree. I told myself I would decorate it tomorrow, but in my heart I knew that was a lie. Truthfully, my mind kept going to January when I would have to carefully take every one of those glass ornaments back off the tree. I just couldn't do it. I decided not to decorate the tree that year. In fact, we decided not to decorate at all. I let the kids have their trees in their rooms, but sans ornaments. We had to cancel family photos twice because of illness, and I let go of that perfect Christmas card picture I had in my head. In fact, I let go of Christmas cards all together.

Four months prior to this, my husband, Kris, had been diagnosed with an autoimmune disease, and we were in the worst of it. I was carrying a lot for my family, and it felt like the weight of everything fell on me. Christmas is my favorite time of year, but this wasn't going to be the Christmas I had dreamed of.

I struggled seeing photos of happy friends all put together for holiday celebrations on social media. Something inside me ached seeing the professional family photos with the sweet smiles and coordinated outfits. It was hard to see pictures from parties and local festivities and to have to continually say "no" to the invitations. I wanted the picture-perfect Christmas, but instead I felt like I was trapped in my own life, looking out the window at the world, wishing my Christmas could be different.

One day, as I shared my frustrations with my friend, Amy, she looked at me and said, "I'm so excited for your family this Christmas. You've been forced to slow down and become laser-focused, and I can't wait to see come January what God did in your hearts and in your family this season."

And slow down we did. Just for good measure, to make sure we weren't tempted to add anything to our schedule, Kris broke a toe. Yep. For real. (And then I won't even go into the stomach bug that ripped its way through our family on Christmas Day.)

But Amy was right. What we were able to focus on was the simple truth of Christmas: Jesus, our Savior, humbling himself, taking all of His holiness and shoving it into human skin, becoming like us, walking this earth, dying on the cross, taking on the full wrath of God, taking our punishment, raising to life on the third day, and defeating death. He did all of this so we could have relationship with God. He didn't merely give us forgiveness and Heaven; He gave us Himself. He didn't sit in Heaven and say, "Get yourself together and perfect, then we will talk about this saving business." Jesus became our Way Maker:

but God shows his love for us in that while we were still sinners,
Christ died for us.
Romans 5:8

And the Word became flesh and dwelt among us, and we have seen his glory,
glory as of the only Son from the Father, full of grace and truth.
John 1:14

That year we weren't caught in the hustle of Christmas. Instead, we slowed down. We did an Advent study as a family. We watched *all* the Christmas movies and read *all* the Christmas books. We had dance parties in our family room. And that bare Christmas tree? As my three young kids brought home Christmas crafts and homemade ornaments, instead of wondering where I'd put them all, they found a home on our tree. By the end of the season, the tree wasn't bare at all. It was covered with sweet reminders from my children that Jesus really was the reason for the season.

Your Christmas may not be the one you hoped for. For some of us, we may be trying to make up for lost time, to fill what was lost with activity and yeses. Can I invite you to a simple Christmas? Despite all that has changed, the simple truth of Christmas remains: Jesus came here. He came to be the Way Maker. I pray this study becomes a guide for you to be able to remember that. I echo Amy's encouragement: allow the simple Christmas to drive your heart to be laser-focused on Jesus, the One who came to give us hope, grace, and mercy.

knowing God

For too many years, I struggled with knowing how to interpret Scripture and apply these ancient words to my life. I did not know that God promises to equip us in studying Scripture through the Holy Spirit. And truthfully, I treated my Bible like one of those balls you shake, ask a question, flip over, and find your answer. Too many times I came to Scripture looking for an answer to my question, or I treated it like a yearbook—looking for all the pictures of myself.

Then, I began asking a different question, and my entire Bible study and life changed. I asked, "What does this say about God?" This shifted my perspective from a self-centered approach toward Scripture (where I am always asking, "What does this mean *to* me or *for* me?") to a God-centered approach—intentionally looking for and seeking out what each passage teaches me about God.

The Bible is not about me. It is first and foremost a book about God, and His name and character are written across every page. Our purpose on earth is to know God and make Him known, to love God and love others. But we can't love what we don't know; we can't worship what we don't know. And the primary way we know God is through His Word. The pursuit of knowledge about God is not optional; it's essential.

On the following pages, you will find two lists to help you: Names of God and Characteristics of God. It's not comprehensive, and there are spaces for you to add others as you discover more with each passage you read. Here are ways you can have a God-centered approach to your study:

- Ask, "What characteristics of God do I see in this passage?"

- Ask, "What names of God do I see in this passage?" (His names speak to His character.)

- Complete this sentence: Because God is _____, I can _____.

I understand there are different roles of the Trinity (God the Father, God the Son, God the Holy Spirit), but for the sake of simplicity (and especially as you are beginning), I think of them as One. If you need further help, visit www.FeastingOnTruth.com for more information and resources.

names of God

Abba Father

Adonai *(Lord, Master)*

Alpha and Omega

Bread of Life

Chief Cornerstone

Creator

Deliverer

El Elyon *(The Most High God)*

El Olam *(The Everlasting God)*

El Roi *(The God Who Sees Me)*

El Shaddai *(The Lord God Almighty)*

Elohim

Everlasting Father

Great High Priest

Holy One

I AM

Immanuel

King of Kings

Lamb of God

Light of the World

Lion of Judah

Lord of Lords

Mighty God

Morning Star

Prince of Peace

Resurrection and the Life

Savior

Wonderful Counselor

Yahweh Amen *(The Lord is Truth)*

Yahweh Jireh *(The Lord Provides)*

Yahweh Nissi *(The Lord is my Banner)*

Yahweh-Raah *(The Lord is my Shepherd)*

Yahweh Rapha *(The Lord Heals)*

Yahweh Shalom *(The Lord is Peace)*

characteristics of God

Abounding in Steadfast Love

Compassionate

Deliberate

Faithful

Forgiving

Full of Grace

Good

Glorious

Gracious

Guide

Holy

Immutable *(Unchanging)*

Infinite

Invisible

Jealous

Just

Kind

Long-Suffering/Patient

Love

Merciful

Mighty

Omnipotent *(All-Powerful)*

Omnipresent

Omniscient *(All-Knowing)*

One

Perfect

Protector

Provider

Refuge/Help

Righteous

Self-Sufficient

Slow to Anger

Sovereign

Trustworthy

Truth

Wise

With Us

KNOWING GOD NOTES

Hebrews

CHAPTER 1

HEBREWS 1 NOTES

KEY VERSES: HEBREWS 1:1–4

Write it out:

Way Maker

HEBREWS 1 NOTES

What does this tell us about Jesus?

_____
_____
_____
_____
_____
_____
_____
_____
_____

How is He the Way Maker?

_____
_____
_____
_____
_____
_____
_____
_____
_____
_____
_____
_____
_____

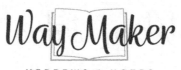

Way Maker

Write a prayer of thanksgiving for who He is:

Go Deeper:

Even when if feels like everything is falling apart, what comfort does it bring to know Jesus holds all things together?

Way Maker

HEBREWS 1 NOTES

Hebrews

CHAPTER 2

KEY VERSES: HEBREWS 2:1,14–18

Write it out:

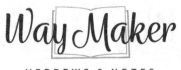

Way Maker

What does this tell us about Jesus?

How is He the Way Maker?

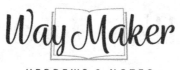

Way Maker

HEBREWS 2 NOTES

Write a prayer of thanksgiving for who He is:

Go Deeper:

Look up *propitiation* in the dictionary and write the definition. How does Jesus do this for us?

....

....

....

....

....

....

....

....

Write out Hebrews 2:1. How can you remember who Jesus is? What does remembering protect you from?

....

....

....

....

....

....

....

....

....

....

....

....

Way Maker

HEBREWS 2 NOTES

Hebrews

CHAPTER 3

KEY VERSES: HEBREWS 3:1–6

Write it out:

Way Maker

HEBREWS 3 NOTES

What does this tell us about Jesus?

How is He the Way Maker?

Way Maker

HEBREWS 3 NOTES

Write a prayer of thanksgiving for who He is:

HEBREWS 3 NOTES

Go Deeper:

How is Jesus the better and more perfect Moses?

Read vv. 7–14. How do we help each other continue to follow Jesus?

Way Maker

HEBREWS 3 NOTES

today

When Kris and I were first married, we were your typical newlyweds: on top of the world and madly in love. When some would see us, they would remark how cute we were. "But just wait," they would say. Once real life settled in . . . when we had kids . . . when we had years behind us . . . that would change. They said the spark would fade.

Well, I, being the uber positive, steadfast girl I am, was annoyed with that. I would show them. Kris and I began to tell ourselves every morning:

> *Someday we may have problems, but it's not going to be today.*

My prayer was that I'd wake up in forty years and still be saying that. *Someday maybe, but not today.* Marriage requires a daily commitment.

Our faith requires us to approach each day with a similar mindset, and the author of Hebrews reminds us to look to Jesus:

> *Therefore, holy brothers, you who share in a heavenly calling, consider Jesus,*
> *the apostle and high priest of our confession, who was faithful to him who*
> *appointed him, just as Moses also was faithful in all God's house.*
> *Hebrews 3:1–2*

The Greek word used for *consider* means "to consider attentively, fix one's eyes or mind upon."[1] In chapter two, he said something similar. He said to pay close attention to Jesus lest we drift away. He's reiterating again to keep looking to Jesus, keep turning your mind to Him, and keep your eyes fixed on Jesus. If we don't, we will naturally move away.

We don't move closer to God on accident. We move closer to God by training our mind to actively stay on Him.

---

1   See https://biblehub.com/greek/2657.htm

Then the author reminds them of a familiar story and a familiar passage:

> *But exhort one another every day, as long as it is called "today," that none of*
> *you may be hardened by the deceitfulness of sin. For we have come to share in*
> *Christ, if indeed we hold our original confidence firm to the end. As it is said,*
> *"Today, if you hear his voice, do not harden your hearts as in the rebellion."*
> *For who were those who heard and yet rebelled? Was it not all those who*
> *left Egypt led by Moses? And with whom was he provoked for forty years?*
> *Was it not with those who sinned, whose bodies fell in the wilderness? And to*
> *whom did he swear that they would not enter his rest, but to those who were*
> *disobedient? So we see that they were unable to enter because of unbelief.*
> *Hebrews 3:13–19*

The Israelites left Egypt bound for Canaan (the Promised Land) on a forty year journey that should have taken eleven days. *Eleven days!* They witnessed the power of God through ten plagues. They saw God's glory in the form of a pillar of cloud by day and a pillar of fire by night. They walked across the Red Sea on *dry* land. They watched walls of water collapse on the army of Pharaoh.

How is it that these people, who saw so many amazing acts of God, could stray so far in their faith that God allowed them to wander the wilderness for forty years and never enter the Promised Land?

They hardened their hearts. Not quickly. Not in an instant. But, over time, they drifted away.

They most likely didn't make a daily choice to honor their commitment. They didn't turn their minds to God. *Every. Day.*

Did you catch what the author said in verse 13? *Today.* Today if you hear His voice, don't harden your hearts. *Today* encourage one another. (He quotes excerpts from Psalm 95 three times.)

What if part of our daily commitment to God is also a daily commitment to each other?

What if we aren't supposed to wait until someone needs encouragement?

What if part of the safeguard against a hardening heart is *daily* encouraging one another to make the commitment every day to say, "Someday I may drift, but it's not going to be today."

Has my faith wavered? You bet. Have I questioned God and wondered why I'm walking the path I am? More than I care to admit. Have I faced hardships? Yes.

Am I in danger of a hardened heart? Unfortunately, yes. We all are. But because of a commitment to my Father, the bumps and twists in the road draw me closer.

Don't miss the Promised Land. Don't miss what God has waiting for you because you drifted and ended up hardening your heart.

Start *today.* Consider Jesus. Turn your mind to Jesus. Fix your mind, your eyes on Jesus. I pray you wake up years from now still saying:

Someday maybe, but not today.

Hebrews

CHAPTER 4

KEY VERSES: HEBREWS 4:14–16

Write it out:

Way Maker

HEBREWS 4 NOTES

What does this tell us about Jesus?

How is He the Way Maker?

Write a prayer of thanksgiving for who He is:

Go Deeper:

How does knowing Jesus suffered everything we suffer bring comfort to you?

Way Maker

HEBREWS 4 NOTES

our great high priest

Tears began falling down my cheeks as my son's teacher shared what happened in class that morning. She explained how the class starts each day with prayer requests and praise reports. The children put their requests up on the board, and when their prayers are answered, they excitedly get to move them from the prayer side to the praise side.

My sweet boy had asked for prayer for his daddy, but as his teacher relayed the words that came next, I couldn't hold those tears back.

"My daddy is sick, but I don't know when we will be able to move him to the praise board. He's going to be sick for a long time."

Maybe you find yourself in a similar situation: a long-term prayer request, a situation that seems endless, a hurt that won't go away, and you are wondering when your prayer requests can move to the praise board. But even on the days that seem rocky, when our dreams are shattered, and we are desperately trying to hold on for dear life, Jesus never leaves our side. Our Great High Priest has been good to us, and this verse has been one of my greatest comforts:

> *Since then we have a great high priest who has passed through the heavens, Jesus, the Son of God, let us hold fast our confession. For we do not have a high priest who is unable to sympathize with our weaknesses, but one who in every respect has been tempted as we are, yet without sin. Let us then with confidence draw near to the throne of grace, that we may receive mercy and find grace to help in time of need.*
> *Hebrews 4:14–16*

Mercy. Grace.

In times of need, God doesn't leave us hanging. He doesn't let us suffer for suffering's sake. He understands our suffering because He too suffered. We can confidently come to Him, and He freely gives us mercy and grace.

In verse 16 above—"find grace to help in time of need"—the Greek word used for *help* is a nautical term and the only other place you see it in the New Testament is in Acts 27:17. Paul was aboard a ship bound for Rome when they encountered a storm. Scripture says, "they used supports to undergird the ship." The word *support* is the same Greek word as *help* used in Hebrews.[1] During storms, sailors would wrap ropes or chains around the boat to literally hold it together as the waves beat against it. That's what *undergird* means: "to strengthen; secure, as by passing a rope or chain under and around."[2]

That is the help available to us. God literally wraps grace and mercy around us to hold us together during the storms of life. When the wind and waves are beating on our lives from all sides, and we fear we aren't going to make it through, His grace holds us together; His mercy supports us; His grace strengthens us; His mercy keeps us secure. It doesn't stop the waves from coming, but it keeps us from falling apart in the storm.

It felt like we were being hit by wave after wave, particularly that Christmas. I was grasping for some sense of control, some semblance of normalcy. I kept trying to hold it together, but I didn't need to hold the pieces together. Jesus was already doing that. His mercy and grace were right there with me, keeping me from falling apart. And He's doing that for you as well.

1   See https://www.blueletterbible.org/lexicon/g996/kjv/tr/0-1/
2   See https://www.blueletterbible.org/lexicon/g5269/kjv/tr/0-1/

Hebrews

CHAPTER 5

Way Maker

HEBREWS 5 NOTES

KEY VERSES: HEBREWS 5:7–10

Write it out:

Way Maker

HEBREWS 5 NOTES

What does this tell us about Jesus?

How is He the Way Maker?

Way Maker

HEBREWS 5 NOTES

Write a prayer of thanksgiving for who He is:

Go Deeper:

Read vv. 1–5. How is Jesus our Great High Priest?

Read Genesis 14:17–24. Who was Melchizedek?

HEBREWS 5 NOTES

Hebrews

CHAPTER 6

HEBREWS 6 NOTES

KEY VERSES: HEBREWS 6:17–20

Write it out:

What does this tell us about Jesus?

How is He the Way Maker?

Way Maker

HEBREWS 6 NOTES

Write a prayer of thanksgiving for who He is: ....

_____

_____

_____

_____

_____

_____

_____

_____

_____

_____

_____

_____

_____

_____

_____

_____

_____

_____

_____

_____

_____

_____

HEBREWS 6 NOTES

Go Deeper:

What characteristics of God the Father are in this passage?

HEBREWS 6 NOTES

hope

My oldest son woke up with a fever; he wouldn't be going to school. I got in the car to take my daughter to school. I turned the key in the ignition. Nothing. We quickly switched to Kris' car and off we went. Later that morning, we tried jumping my car. The battery wouldn't charge. Kris, who during this time was at the height of his battle against an autoimmune disease, drove to the auto store—it was a bad battery and thankfully under warranty. He drove back home, but when he tried to put the battery in, he realized the guy at the store gave him the wrong one. By now, there wasn't enough time for him to go back to exchange the battery. So later, when I got home from picking up our daughter, Kris immediately left to exchange the battery. He ran into some pretty heavy construction traffic. It was too much, so he turned around and came home. With all of the extra running around, we hadn't been able to go to the grocery store, so dinner was an interesting mix. Finally, we gave up on getting to the auto store that night. Kris went to pull his car into the garage to discover he now had a flat tire. We called the shop. They didn't have an opening for three days. My two-year-old poured his milk on the couch. My seven-year-old was on the verge of tears because he just didn't feel well. Kris and I were done.

You've probably had days like these—where nothing seems to go right and you're exhausted, beat down, D-O-N-E; all you want to do is crawl into bed and get the day over with.

We decided to put the kids to bed early because we had nothing left. I went into my four-year-old daughter's room. She bounded across her room, grabbed her purple Bible, and plopped down on the floor. "I need to read to my little friends, Mommy." I was so tempted in my exhaustion to say no, that she needed to brush her teeth and get to bed. But instead, I let her. She opened her Bible, flipping the pages. "I have to find the right one" (flip, flip, flip); "here it is!" Then she said, "I don't know the story, but I can sing the words!" And she started to speak/sing, "Away in a manger, no crib for a bed, the little Lord Jesus lay down His sweet head. The stars in the sky look down where He lay. The little Lord Jesus asleep on the hay."

With a sigh and a smile, I looked down at her Bible and saw the title page for 1 Kings, and I felt Him whisper: "I am the *one King*. And I'm still on the throne."

Our King Jesus came here. He didn't come as a great ruler, into a wealthy family, a palace, or even a nice suburban home. He didn't even have a crib. He lost his father. He lost a friend. He withstood false accusations. He suffered. He was hungry. He resisted temptation. He wept. His friends abandoned Him. He endured beatings. Jesus came to die. He came for us. He came to give us hope. And not just any hope:

> *We have this as a sure and steadfast anchor of the soul, a hope that enters into*
> *the inner place behind the curtain, where Jesus has gone as a forerunner on*
> *our behalf, having become a high priest forever after the order of Melchizedek.*
> *Hebrews 6:19–20*

Melchizedek was a king, but also a high priest in Salem (for more, see Genesis 14). Here, the author of Hebrews points us to this story because Jesus is the more perfect Melchizedek: both King and High Priest. And Jesus, being our Great High Priest, went behind the curtain—the place where only the earthly high priest could go once a year to make a sacrifice and ask forgiveness for the sins of all people, the place where God's glory dwelled—and became the intermediary for us. And because Jesus did that for us, we have hope. But not just fluffy, wishful thinking, fairy dust, wavering, "gee, it sure would be nice if that happened" hope. *Sure, steadfast, anchoring* hope.

This hope is what holds us firmly in place. Like an anchor secures a ship, keeping it from drifting away, so is the truth that Jesus went on our behalf and did what no other high priest had done before: secured our position *eternally* with our Father. I should also mention that *Salem* is Hebrew for "peace", and most scholars believe this city was in the same location as Jerusalem. So, not only is Jesus an anchor of hope for eternity, but He came, ultimately sacrificing Himself in the city of peace, so that we may have peace for eternity too.

> *I have said these things to you, that in me you may have peace. In the world*
> *you will have tribulation. But take heart; I have overcome the world.*
> *John 16:33*

Oh sweet friends, I don't know where you are today. I don't know what trouble you might be facing. But I do know this: Jesus is with you. Take heart. He has overcome. He is anchoring you with hope and covering you with peace. He is our one King, Great High Priest, and He is holding you in place. And that is a hope that will not disappoint.

Hebrews

CHAPTER 7

HEBREWS 7 NOTES

KEY VERSES: HEBREWS 7:22-28

Write it out:

Way Maker

HEBREWS 7 NOTES

What does this tell us about Jesus?

How is He the Way Maker?

Write a prayer of thanksgiving for who He is:

Go Deeper:

How is the sacrifice Jesus offered better and more perfect than the one the priests used to offer?

HEBREWS 7 NOTES

Hebrews

CHAPTER 8

KEY VERSES: HEBREWS 8:1–7

Write it out:

HEBREWS 8 NOTES

What does this tell us about Jesus?

How is He the Way Maker?

HEBREWS 8 NOTES

Write a prayer of thanksgiving for who He is:

Go Deeper:

What is the definition of the word *shadow*?

How are the old sacrificial system and the temple a shadow pointing us to Jesus?

HEBREWS 8 NOTES

Hebrews

CHAPTER 9

KEY VERSES: HEBREWS 9:11–14; 24–28

Write it out:

Way Maker

What does this tell us about Jesus?

How is He the Way Maker?

Way Maker

HEBREWS 9 NOTES

Write a prayer of thanksgiving for who He is:

Go Deeper:

What hope do we have for eternity because of Jesus making the way?

Way Maker

HEBREWS 9 NOTES

Hebrews

CHAPTER 10

KEY VERSES: HEBREWS 10:19–25

Write it out:

Way Maker

HEBREWS 10 NOTES

What does this tell us about Jesus?

How is He the Way Maker?

Way Maker

HEBREWS 10 NOTES

Write a prayer of thanksgiving for who He is:

Go Deeper:

How should we respond because of what Jesus did for us?

Way Maker

HEBREWS 10 NOTES

who does that?!

Some women come into your life, and you are never the same for it. Lynda was one of those women. It was an unlikely friendship. Her kids and I grew up in school together, and she always loved to tell people how she had known me since I was knee-high (which was funny because I grew to be about eight inches taller than Lynda!). We worked together at the same church, and I led a Bible study during our lunch break. It started large, but eventually it dwindled down to just Lynda and me. We would meet one morning a week before work to study God's Word together. Today, she is one of the reasons I love His Word so much.

Every step of the way, Lynda was there. When God called me to start Feasting on Truth, Lynda was still right there—praying, showing up, even leading groups when I asked. (Which, I might add, she always did reluctantly. Lynda thought she was better at leading children than she was at leading women. This was not true at all.) She had a way with words, and she used them generously to encourage others—no matter what age they happened to be.

The years 2020 and 2021 brought losses for many of us: jobs, dreams, plans, people. Lynda was one of my great losses. She passed away on September 12, 2021. I know the moment she breathed her last here and experienced the wholeness of Heaven, she was probably tracking down John to thank him for penning her life verse (John 16:33) and looking for Peter and Paul, asking them *all* the questions.

Lynda had such an incredible perspective of our Way Maker. In Bible study, she would often exclaim, "Who does that?!" as we witnessed the incredible kindness of our God. Our studies were full of those moments: when Jesus would go out of His way to meet a woman at a well or step out in a garden to face those who came to arrest Him saying, "Here I AM." She would inevitably say, "Who does that?!" Only Jesus. And she knew Him well.

Hebrews 10 is one big "Who does that?!" passage.

We have a God who gave us a picture of what He was going to do (a shadow) and was faithful to follow through. The author of Hebrews calls the law a *shadow* of the true form. A shadow is not something to grab or hold. A shadow is just a darkened outline of an object. It's not the real thing; it's a representation of the real thing. He is comparing what the priests had to do to ask forgiveness for sins (the shadow) to how Christ died once for all (the true form).

One time each year, the high priest (and only the high priest) would enter the presence of God and offer a sacrifice to ask forgiveness for the sins of Israel for that year (see Leviticus 16). The presence of God dwelled in the Tabernacle and later in Solomon's temple in what was called the Holy of Holies or the Most Holy Place. This area was at the heart of the Tabernacle and the temple, and it was sectioned off by a huge curtain (or veil). While the Bible doesn't say how large or thick the curtain was, tradition suggests it was about fifteen to eighteen feet high and was as thick as your hand. But all of that was a shadow. The real Savior was coming!

My favorite part of the redemption story comes just as Jesus breathes His last on the cross:

> *Now from the sixth hour there was darkness over all the land until the ninth hour. And about the ninth hour Jesus cried out with a loud voice, saying, "Eli, Eli, lema sabachthani?" that is, "My God, my God, why have you forsaken me?" . . . And Jesus cried out again with a loud voice and yielded up his spirit. And behold, the curtain of the temple was torn in two, from top to bottom. And the earth shook, and the rocks were split.*
> *Matthew 27:45–46; 50–51*

The moment Jesus died, the tall curtain that couldn't be torn tore from top to bottom. No one cut it; it was not ripped by human hands. God, through Jesus, made a way for us to have intimate access to Him like never before.

Who does that?!

> *Therefore, brothers, since we have confidence to enter the holy places by the blood of Jesus, by the new and living way that he opened for us through the curtain, that is, through his flesh, and since we have a great priest over the house of God, let us draw near with a true heart in full assurance of faith, with our hearts sprinkled clean from an evil conscience and our bodies washed with pure water.*
> *Hebrews 10:19–22*

We no longer have to stand at a distance! His body, pierced and torn, opened a way for us to draw near. His blood gives us confidence to enter "the holy places." We no longer have to get cleaned up before we can come to God. He meets us where we are. Once and for all, His sacrifice accomplished what years of sacrifices (plural) could never do: forgiveness of sins (Hebrews 10:17–18), finished the work (Hebrews 10:12–14), and made us clean (Hebrews 10:22–23).

I will never get over what He did for me. I don't get it. I do not deserve His grace, forgiveness, and love. I continually find myself returning to the same pit of sin; and every time, He meets me there, pulls me out and says, "I forgive you. I love you. No matter what."

Who does that?!

Don't settle for the shadow of Christianity. Not one of us is good enough to do it on our own. And there is no life He cannot redeem. No one is too far gone. That curtain tore in two so we could draw near to our Creator with confidence. I pray this Christmas you draw close and find time to reflect on what His coming means for us as believers. Hold fast to that confession of hope without wavering.

And because He did that, don't miss His call to community either:

Let us hold fast the confession of our hope without wavering, for he who promised is faithful. And let us consider how to stir up one another to love and good works, not neglecting to meet together, as is the habit of some, but encouraging one another, and all the more as you see the Day drawing near.
Hebrews 10:23–25

I will always be grateful that Lynda never stopped stirring others up toward love and good works. The line of people with a testimony of how she showed up for them, encouraged them, and met with them, is long. She kept pointing people to our "Who Does That?!" God. Even when our study dwindled to two, she didn't neglect to show up. Even when she was walking through some hard things, she kept being obedient to God's call. That's the kind of woman I want to be. It's my prayer for you too. Let's keep showing up because when we needed it most, our Way Maker showed up for us.

Who does that?!

Hebrews

CHAPTER 11

Way Maker

HEBREWS 11 NOTES

KEY VERSES: HEBREWS 11:1-3, 6

Write it out:

Way Maker

HEBREWS 11 NOTES

What does this tell us about Jesus?

How is He the Way Maker?

HEBREWS 11 NOTES

Write a prayer of thanksgiving for who He is:

Way Maker

HEBREWS 11 NOTES

Go Deeper:

What is the definition of *faith*?

Pick two or three of the names mentioned in this "Hall of Faith" and look up their stories. What hope do you have because of their testimonies?

Way Maker

HEBREWS 11 NOTES

Hebrews

CHAPTER 12

Way Maker

HEBREWS 12 NOTES

KEY VERSES: HEBREWS 12:1–2, 22–29

Write it out:

Way Maker

HEBREWS 12 NOTES

What does this tell us about Jesus?

How is He the Way Maker?

Write a prayer of thanksgiving for who He is:

Go Deeper:

Read Mark 13:24–27. What hope do you have in knowing His kingdom cannot be shaken?

Way Maker

HEBREWS 12 NOTES

the shaking

I felt like I was herding cats. The hands of my kids (ages two, four, and seven) were moving faster than I could manage. My husband was at home in bed resting, and there I was at my parents' house trying to make Christmas cookies with my children. I wanted to teach them how you carefully place each cookie cutter near the edge to get the most out of the dough. Instead, cookie cutters were haphazardly smooshed wherever their hearts desired. I was frantically jumping in as cut pieces of dough were carelessly picked up and thrown onto the cookie sheet. Stars were misshaped. Hearts were squished. Gingerbread men were losing their heads. I was about to lose my mind.

That was how I felt about my life right then: I was frantically trying to manage it all, but I couldn't. Balls kept dropping. Everything seemed out of my control. I could not hold it all together—not even the poor gingerbread men.

That was a year of shaking for me. I felt God shaking me as the waves of hardship, trials, setbacks, and unknowns continued to pound. With each wave, things began spilling out of me, and they weren't pretty. The shaking revealed the ugly sin in my heart. Until those days, I had fancied myself a "good girl." But as my trials continued on, God continued to shake out of me what could be shaken—all for the purpose of showing me what cannot be shaken.

At that time his voice shook the earth, but now he has promised, "Yet once
more I will shake not only the earth but also the heavens." This phrase,
"Yet once more," indicates the removal of things that are shaken—that
is, things that have been made—in order that the things that cannot be
shaken may remain.
Hebrews 12:26–27

John Newton, who wrote the hymn "Amazing Grace", often wrote letters to parishioners to encourage them in their faith and encourage them through their hardships. In his book *Newton on the Christian Life*, Tony Reinke points to Newton's idea that trials smoke out our idols.

In other words, trials are designed to prevent us from living at peace with our
idols and remaining in sin. Much of our sin appears hidden and dormant un-
til the whip-snap of affliction rouses the indwelling sin to stand up and show
itself, or stand up and hiss, or stand up and strike. It is more necessary for us to
see the sins remaining in our hearts and to flee to Christ for grace than it is to
live blissfully ignorant of the cancers in our soul. And we know this, Newton
explains, because God sends afflictions into our lives. Trials are medicines of
kindness applied to serious diseases called indwelling sins.[1]

Idol work has been a hard yet necessary practice in my relationship with God. An idol is anything we value more than God and anything we turn to instead of God. It can be something physical, an action, or even an emotion.

That Christmas began to reveal to me how much value I had placed on the events and traditions of Christmas over the Author of Christmas. It reminded me that He is sovereign over it all. It reminded me that He does not ask me to hold everything together; He is already doing that. It reminded me that I do not need to know the future; I need to remember that He goes before me and behind me. He hems me in.

Instead, He asks me to throw off all that hinders me; to let go of the weights that hold me down and run with endurance after Him (Hebrews 12:1–2). Sometimes throwing off what hinders me comes at the hands of trials. It comes in times of suffering. It comes with shaking.

I have a love-hate relationship with the word *endurance*, but we are called to it (or your version may say *perseverance*) over and over in Scripture. The Greek word for *endurance* means "steadfast, patiently waiting."[2] It comes from two root words meaning "under" and "remain".

I don't want to stay under. I want to bypass the hurt. I want to skirt around the pain. I want to get out from under the hardships. But that's not what we are called to do. Like the old children's story tells us, we can't go over it. We can't go under it. We can't go around it. We have to go through it. The only way through is through. But God continues to use these hardships to grow me, to build endurance, to refine my character; and the result is hope (Romans 5:3–5). That's what Christmas is all about: hope. Not a wish or a flimsy desire or something arbitrary. It's that Hebrews 6, sure and steadfast hope—hope that does not disappoint or put us to shame. Hope that

1   Reinke, T. (2015). *Newton on the Christian Life: To Live Is Christ.* United States: Crossway. p. 182
2   See https://biblehub.com/greek/5281.htm

one day, we will be in eternity with Christ. There will be no more tears or death or mourning or weeping or pain. Hope that all things will be made new. God will dwell with us and us with Him.

What remains true and what cannot be shaken are the things of God. What a glorious promise! And, as the author of Hebrews says, our response is worship. We are grateful. We are in awe of our God, who made a way through Jesus for us to receive that which is unchanging and unmovable and unshakable (Hebrews 12:28–29). And let's face it: we were going to bite the head of the gingerbread man off anyway.

Hebrews

CHAPTER 13

HEBREWS 13 NOTES

KEY VERSES: HEBREWS 13:20-21

Write it out:

Way Maker

HEBREWS 13 NOTES

What does this tell us about Jesus?

_____
_____
_____
_____
_____
_____
_____
_____
_____
_____

How is He the Way Maker?

_____
_____
_____
_____
_____
_____
_____
_____
_____
_____
_____
_____
_____

Write a prayer of thanksgiving for who He is:

Go Deeper:

Read the entire chapter. Because of who He is and how He has made a way, how should our life look different?

Way Maker

HEBREWS 13 NOTES

remember

Over and over in Scripture, we see God call His people to remember. They built a stone altar to remember crossing the Jordan. The Israelites carry a jar of manna to remember God's provision in the wilderness. They celebrate Passover to remember God saving them from Egypt. We celebrate the Lord's Supper to remember Christ's death on the cross. Recording and remembering is an important practice in our faith. It's how we can look back and see where God worked in our lives and how we've changed as a result.

One of my favorite times to remember is at the end of the calendar year. I love to look back on the year. As the saying goes, hindsight is 20/20, and it's often at the end of the year I can look back and see how far God took me during those last twelve months. These next pages are a guide—a way for you to reflect on the past year and see the hand of God.

It can be hard to do this, but thankfully God doesn't call us to remember without providing the help we need to do so. In John 14:26, Jesus promises, "But the Helper, the Holy Spirit, whom the Father will send in my name, he will teach you all things and bring to your remembrance all that I have said to you." The Holy Spirit is there to guide you and help you remember.

You do not have to work through the following pages all at once. I recommend getting away, if even for an hour, to a quiet place with no distractions. Our tendency in these types of exercises is to focus on the physical things God did or what He physically or materially gave us. But I challenge you to use the list of God's names and characteristics on pages 12–13. Where did you see Him display His character in your life? Where did you see His grace, goodness, gentleness, patience, etc.?

The older I get, the more I realize life is not a series of peaks and valleys but rather a dance between joy and sorrow. They can, and often do, coexist. Good and hard are not mutually exclusive. Even in the midst of hard years, I know God never ceased being God. As my friend, Amy, says, "Find Jesus in the junk." Pray. Invite the Holy Spirit to help you remember and bring to mind who God is and what He has done for you.

REMEMBER

REMEMBER LIFE

What was hard this year?

REMEMBER

What was good this year?

What memories do I want to remember?

REMEMBER

REMEMBER HABITS

What did I stop doing that I do not want to start again?

What did I start doing that I do not want to stop?

REMEMBER

REMEMBER GOD

How did God surprise me this year?

REMEMBER

How did God provide for me this year?

How did God change my perspective this year?

REMEMBER

How did God show His character in my life this year?

REMEMBER

REFLECT BACK/LOOK FORWARD

What was my word/goal for this year? What did God teach me?

REMEMBER

What is my word/goal for next year? Why?

REMEMBER

feasting at the table

There's something about Christmas that screams cookies. I can remember as a young girl baking cookies with four generations: my great-grandmother (pictured left), my grand-mother, my mom, and us kids. We made the same family recipes year after year: buckeye balls, jam dots, sugar cookies, and gingerbread cookies. It's a tradition we've continued to carry on now for more years than I can count. I love passing on these recipes to my own children.

Food evokes memories. I can take one bite of a buckeye ball and instantly be taken back to Christmas-cookie baking. There's something powerful about being in the kitchen together, working together, and eating together. It creates a sense of belonging. It draws people together. And at the end of the process, there's something (hopefully) delicious to enjoy. (If not, maybe you'll get a good #kitchenfail story out of it.) But all this seems to be exponentially increased during family holidays.

My favorite cookies are chocolate ones, but a few Christmases ago I discovered peppermint chips—and these Dark Chocolate Peppermint Cookies were born. I mean, what could be more Christmas than peppermint and chocolate?! They are delicate and surprisingly light. The re-freshing peppermint balances the richness of the dark chocolate, and they are now my husband's favorite cookie. Because they are chocolate, it's hard to tell when they are done. Every oven is different, but mine is precisely eight and a half minutes. If you're unsure, after removing them from the oven let them sit on the tray for a couple minutes before moving to the cooling rack.

This recipe makes about four dozen cookies, so feel free to share. You can freeze the extra cook-ies (*if* you have any). Enjoy, and happy feasting!

DARK CHOCOLATE PEPPERMINT COOKIES

Time: About 45 minutes
Yield: About 48 small cookies

INGREDIENTS

2 cups unbleached all-purpose flour
1 teaspoon baking soda
1 teaspoon baking powder
½ teaspoon salt
½ cup unsweetened cocoa powder

1 cup unsalted butter, softened
1 ¼ c sugar
2 tablespoons molasses
2 eggs
1 teaspoon vanilla

1 bag peppermint chips
1 bag dark chocolate chips

flake sea salt

INSTRUCTIONS

1. Preheat the oven to 375 degrees. Line two cookie sheets with parchment paper.

2. In a medium bowl, whisk together flour, baking soda, baking powder, salt, and cocoa powder. Set aside.

3. In the bowl of a stand mixer with paddle attachment, cream the butter and sugar at medium-high speed until light and fluffy, about 3 minutes. (If you do not have a stand mixer, you can use a hand mixer instead.)

4. Reduce speed to low. Add molasses, scraping down the sides of the bowl.

5. Add the eggs, one at a time, mixing well. Then add the vanilla.

6. With the mixer still on low, gradually add the flour mixture, scraping down the sides of the bowl periodically.

7. Turn off mixer, remove bowl, and thoroughly stir in the chocolate and peppermint chips.

8. Spoon dough onto cookie sheets about 2–3 inches apart using a tablespoon cookie scoop (about the size of a dinner spoon). Gently press the top of each cookie so it's flat. Sprinkle with flake sea salt. You should be able to fit about 12 cookies per sheet.

9. Bake at 375 degrees for 8–9 minutes. Let cool on tray for about 4 minutes before moving to a cooling rack. Repeat with the remaining dough.

about Erin

ERIN H. WARREN is passionate about equipping and encouraging women to discover God's truths for themselves. She is the author of *Feasting on Truth: Savor the Life-giving Word of God*, leads and teaches Bible study through her ministry Feasting on Truth, and has published several Bible studies. She and her husband, Kris, have three littles (who aren't so little anymore), and they live in Central Florida. She loves a house full of people and a table full of food and hopes tacos never go out of style. You can find more information about Feasting on Truth on her website: FeastingOnTruth.com. You can also connect with her on Instagram: @erinhwarren and @feastingontruth and YouTube: www.youtube.com/c/erinhwarren.

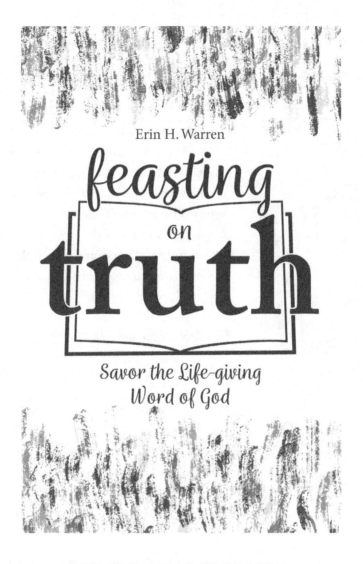

FEASTING ON TRUTH

SAVOR THE LIFE-GIVING WORD OF GOD

The Word of God is our very life, but Erin Warren felt anything but alive. Her husband was sick. Her world was falling apart, and she had questions. Feel-good faith was not enough; she needed deep, sustaining truths.

Through her own wrestling, Erin Warren addresses the obstacles that held her back when it came to Bible study and how she discovered to savor the life-giving Word of God.

The word *feast* is rooted in abundance. That is what awaits us in the pages of Scripture: a table laid out before us, not only for our essential nourishment, but for our enjoyment.

FeastingOnTruth.com/Books

STORIES FROM THE WILDERNESS

A STUDY OF THE ISRAELITES' JOURNEY FROM EGYPT TO THE PROMISED LAND

The wilderness. It is a place that feels hard, empty, lifeless, and pathless, and it often leaves us with questions about who God is. But where we see a place that is worthless, confusing, and chaotic, God sees a place to display His power. Time and time again throughout Scripture, God takes the worthless, seemingly wasteful, confusing, chaotic, and empty places and uses them as a backdrop to prove His character, draw us in, and display His glory.

FeastingOnTruth.com/Wilderness

TO DWELL IN OUR MIDST

A STUDY OF THE TABERNACLE AND HOW IT POINTS US TO JESUS

Why study this ancient tent? What does knowing about the Tabernacle have to do with our faith on this side of the cross? Everything. This tent is not merely ritual or history or good information—it's essential to understanding our salvation. Our detailed and deliberate God gave us the Tabernacle because one day, He would give us Jesus. It's an invitation into a relationship with our Holy God. Discover God's plan to dwell in our midst through Jesus Christ.

FeastingOnTruth.com/Dwell

LIGHT AND LIFE

AN INDUCTIVE BIBLE STUDY ON PSALM 119

We hear it all the time: we need to read the Bible every day. But why is it so important that we know, understand, and apply this ancient book to our lives today? What's in it for us? In Psalm 119, we see over and over that God's Word brings life, and it's a light to guide us. If we truly knew the power the Word of God has in our lives, we wouldn't be able to put it down.

FeastingOnTruth.com/LightAndLife

BY HIS GRACE FOR HIS GLORY

AN INDUCTIVE STUDY ON THE BOOK OF ROMANS

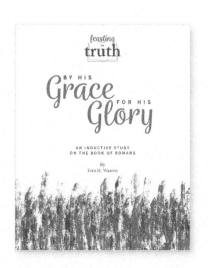

Romans is foundational yet deep. It's hard to understand yet simple. It is an incredibly powerful book that has been changing lives for centuries, and the truths in these sixteen chapters have the power to change our faith too. There are many familiar verses in Romans, and we associate this book with evangelism. But it is so much more! Discover what it looks like to live by His grace for His glory.

FeastingOnTruth.com/Romans

UNEXPECTED SAVIOR

AN INDUCTIVE BIBLE STUDY ON THE GOSPEL OF MARK

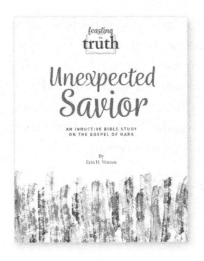

The Gospel of Mark challenges the expected ideal of the Messiah—not a conquering king or a wish-granting genie, but rather a man of sorrows and a suffering servant. This short yet impactful account of Jesus' life reveals the character of the One who came to save us. Jesus mourned the brokenness around Him: the sickness, the pain, the hardness of heart. He grew angry at the sin of those who led His sheep astray. He was the One who came not to be served, but to serve. He came to prove the faithfulness of God and provide unshakable hope as we walk through hardships.

FeastingOnTruth.com/Mark